A SHORT BIOGRAPHY OF ERNEST HEMINGWAY

A SHORT BIOGRAPHY OF

Ernest Hemingway

Henri-Pierre Corbacho

Carlisle, Massachusetts

A Short Biography of Ernest Hemingway

Series Editor: Susan DeLand
Written by: Henri-Pierre Corbacho

For My Beloved Parents

978-1-944038-53-3

FRONT COVER: *Portrait of Ernest Hemingway,* 1929
Waldo Peirce (American, 1884–1970)
Oil on canvas
Ernest Hemingway Collection
John F. Kennedy Presidential Library and Museum, Boston, MA
Photography credit: Joel Benjamin
Copyright maintained by artist's estate

BACK COVER: *Ernest Hemingway writing in camp on Safari in Kenya,* 1953
Earl Theisen (American, 1903–1973)
Photograph
© Earl Theisen Archives
Photograph in the Ernest Hemingway Photograph Collection
John F. Kennedy Presidential Library and Museum, Boston, MA
Courtesy of Roxann E. Livingston

Published by Benna Books
an imprint of Applewood Books, Inc.
Carlisle, Massachusetts

To request a free copy of our current catalog
featuring our best-selling books, write to:
Applewood Books, Inc.
P.O. Box 27
Carlisle, Massachusetts 01741
Or visit us on the web at: www.awb.com

10 9 8 7 6 5 4 3 2 1
MANUFACTURED IN THE UNITED STATES OF AMERICA

THE GREAT FIRE OF 1871 PROMPTED many Chicago residents to resettle in Cicero, Illinois, a conservative and mainly Protestant upper-middle-class suburb, later to become Oak Park. On July 21, 1899, the town saw the birth of one who would become its most celebrated resident, Ernest Miller Hemingway, American novelist, journalist, short-story writer, winner of the 1953 Pulitzer Prize and the 1954 Nobel Prize in Literature, and legendary for his adventurous and widely publicized life.

The second of six children, Ernest was the first son of Clarence Edmonds Hemingway, a puritanical physician with a love for the outdoors, and Grace Hall Hemingway, an opera singer and music teacher. The family lived in a large home with a medical office for Clarence and a music studio for Grace. They also owned a small cottage called Windemere in Walloon Lake, Michigan, where Ernest spent summers with his four sisters—Marcelline, Ursula, Madelaine, and Carol—and his brother, Leicester. During that time, the young, inquisitive boy learned from his father how to hunt, fish, camp, shoot, and appreciate the outdoors. These experiences had a profound effect on him and prepared him for a life of adventures and discoveries.

Hemingway described his hometown as having "wide lawns and narrow minds."

Ernest's relationship with his mother was quite uncommon. Grace was domineering and capable of disquieting bouts of irresponsibility. When Ernest was a baby she would hold him in her arms while shooting a revolver. She would also dress him and his older sister, Marcelline, as twins, calling him Ernestine. She insisted that he learn how to play the cello, which he profoundly disliked. As an adult, Hemingway admitted that he hated his mother. When she died in Oak Park in 1951, he did not attend her funeral. His father, Clarence, who suffered from severe diabetes and heart disease, had also endured her abuse. Depressed and having experienced significant financial losses in the Florida real estate market, Clarence committed suicide in 1928. This tragedy had a profound effect on Hemingway and his siblings and greatly influenced his writing.

When Hemingway learned of his father's suicide, he commented: "I'll probably go the same way."

While attending Oak Park and River Forest High School, Ernest joined the water polo, football, track and field, and boxing teams and wrote sports articles for the school newspaper, *Trapeze and Tabula*. He was a good student, excelling in English classes. He also played the cello in the school orchestra with Marcelline. After graduation in 1916, Ernest did not enter college but went to Kansas City to begin his career as a cub reporter for the *Kansas City Star,* an experience he admitted influenced his writing style. His concise, eloquent prose and the intense virility of his writing would influence twentieth-century American and British fiction.

Hemingway said: "Newspaper work will not harm a young writer and could help him if he gets out of it in time."

The United States entered the First World War and Hemingway was rejected from military service due to his poor vision. He joined the war effort as an ambulance driver for the American Red Cross in Italy. At a munitions factory explosion in Milan, Hemingway witnessed for the first time the carnage and horrors of war. He described the event in his book *Death in the Afternoon.* No American writer has written more about war in the twentieth century than Hemingway. On July 8, 1918, only eighteen years old, he was seriously wounded by mortar fire on the Austro-Italian front while running a motorized canteen offering cigarettes and sweets to soldiers. It left shrapnel in both his legs. Although injured, Hemingway helped a wounded Italian soldier and was hit again in the legs by several bullets. He was awarded the Silver Medal of Valor from the Italian government. He received treatment for his injury at a field hospital before being transferred to a Red Cross hospital in Milan, where he remained for six months. While recuperating, Hemingway met and fell in love with a Red Cross nurse named Agnes von Kurowsky. She accepted his proposal of marriage but a few month later declined to marry him, stating that she had become engaged to an Italian officer.

A piece of shrapnel is on display at the JFK Presidential Library, which holds the Hemingway Collection.

Devastated and still nursing his injury, Hemingway returned to northern Michigan in 1919. Compared to the life-changing events he had experienced during the war, Hemingway found his new existence dull.

His wartime experiences formed the basis for his novel *A Farewell to Arms*.

During a camping trip with friends in Michigan, he found inspiration for *Big Two-Hearted River*, in which the returning-from-war main character finds peace in nature. Hemingway then accepted a position at the *Toronto Star Weekly* as a foreign correspondent.

While visiting friends in Chicago, he met and fell in love with St. Louis native Elizabeth Hadley Richardson. Hadley was a shy, red-haired woman. Born in 1891, she was eight years older than Hemingway. She received her education at Bryn Mawr College, a Pennsylvania private women's liberal arts institution. After a courtship of less than a year, they married on September 3, 1921, in Horton Bay, Michigan, and honeymooned on Walloon Lake. There were surprising similarities between her family and Hemingway's: Her mother was a talented musician and singer. Her father worked for a pharmaceutical company, and after facing financial difficulties, he also committed suicide.

Ernest and Hadley moved to Paris, where it was said "the most interesting people in the world live."

Hadley would be the first of Hemingway's four wives. They moved to Paris and settled in a small, run-down apartment in the Left Bank's Latin Quarter, living a bohemian lifestyle.

Hemingway continued writing for the *Toronto Star,* covering events such as the Geneva Conference and the Greco-Turkish war, witnessing the plight of thousands of Greek refugees. He documented one of the hidden costs of war, the dislodgment of people from their original countries. Hemingway met American expatriate, poet, and critic Ezra Pound, who invited him to meet Gertrude Stein. Hemingway would develop a lifelong friendship with both. Stein, who had moved to Paris in 1903, was an American writer and poet known for her modernist views, art collection, and penchant for hosting friends in her literary salon. She introduced Hemingway to what she famously called "the lost generation," a group of expatriate artists and writers of the 1920s. This circle of modernists, including F. Scott Fitzgerald, Ezra Pound, Pablo Picasso, and Joan Miró, inspired and influenced the young writer. He was also motivated by Russian authors Leo Tolstoy, Fyodor Dostoevsky,

Joyce would start bar brawls and then have Hemingway beat the person up.

and Anton Chekhov. Hemingway would often join in alcoholic binges with his friend the Irish novelist and poet James Joyce.

> *"The good parts of a book may be only something a writer is lucky enough to overhear or it may be the wreck of his whole damn life—and one is as good as the other."*

In September 1923, Ernest and his wife returned to Toronto. Their son, John Hadley Nicanor Hemingway, was born on October 10, 1923. The baby was named for his mother and for Nicanor Villalta y Serrés, a Spanish bullfighter Hemingway admired. As a child, John was affectionately called "Bumby" by his parents, though his father often called him "Schatz," German for treasure. John, later known as Jack, inherited his mother's conviviality and friendly character and his father's physique. That same year, Hemingway's first book, *Three Stories and Ten Poems*, was published, followed by *In Our Time*.

Hemingway quickly found life in Toronto monotonous, and in January 1924 he and his family returned to Paris. When Hadley and Ernest lived in Paris and went out at night, they would leave Bumby in the care of their cat, "Featherpussy."

> *"I can't think of any better way to spend money than on Champagne."*

In 1925 the couple traveled to Spain, joined by a group of American and British expatriates. He began to be referred to as "Papa." Hemingway became fascinated by bullfighting. They visited Pamplona and the legendary Festival of San Fermin, the basis for his famous novel *The Sun Also Rises*. A literary chef d'oeuvre and a classic example of his commanding writing style, the novel is believed to be his greatest work and established Hemingway as one of the most prominent writers of the century.

The novel is a poignant observation of the disillusionment and anguish of the post–World War I generation.

In 1926, Hadley realized that Hemingway was having an affair with

Vanity Fair and *Vogue* American journalist Pauline Marie Pfeiffer, whom he had met in Paris. The couple were divorced in early 1927 and Hadley remained in France until 1934. Young Jack was raised by his mother after his parents divorced, seeing his father only during summer vacations. Hadley then moved to London and married American journalist Paul Mowrer before returning to America. She died in Lakeland, Florida, in 1979.

Pauline Marie Pfeiffer was born in Iowa in 1895, in a devout Catholic and wealthy family. Her father was a landowner in Arkansas, and her uncles made their fortune in the pharmaceutical and cosmetics industries. Pauline was raised in St. Louis, where she graduated from the University of Missouri School of Journalism. In Paris, she lived in a tastefully decorated Right Bank apartment and wore elegant dresses and fashionable jewelry created by the trendiest French designers. By contrast, Hemingway was

Pauline was bright and glamorous and showed a great sense of humor.

struggling to support himself, living in a small, cold flat, and would at times skip meals to make ends meet. Hemingway converted to Catholicism and married Pauline in May 1927. They honeymooned in Le Grau-du-Roi in southern France. That same year, *Men without Women,* a collection of fourteen stories focusing on the casualties of war, relationships between men and women, and sportsmanship, was published.

By the end of the year, Pauline became pregnant and the couple decided to move back to America. In 1928, their son Patrick Hemingway was born in Kansas City. Patrick spent his first years traveling to Europe with his parents. He lived in Key West when the family moved to Florida, where he was tended by staff—Ada and Isabel. Patrick often visited his father in Cuba after his parents divorced. The family spent their summers in Wyoming. Hemingway fell in love with the American West, which he called "the most beautiful country I have seen."

The highly acclaimed *A Farewell to Arms* was published in 1929. Set on the Italian front, the semiautobiographical story recounts the doomed love affair between a wounded American ambulance officer and a beautiful English nurse.

Hemingway rewrote the ending of *A Farewell to Arms* thirty-nine times to get the words right.

On November 12, 1931, Hemingway's third son and last child, Gregory Hancock Hemingway, was born in Kansas City. When Gregory, nicknamed "Gig," reached his late teens, he and his father became estranged. Father and son kept a strained relationship for many years.

The family spent their winters in Florida. The house, where Hemingway had his writing studio, was nestled in the heart of Old Town Key West and would be home for the next ten years. When his sons played outside, Ernest could be heard bellowing from his study window for them to be quiet. The house was conveniently located across from the lighthouse, guiding Hemingway home after drinking sprees at Sloppy Joe's, the neighborhood bar. Now the Hemingway

Home Museum, it is also home to six- and seven-toed cats, all descendants of Hemingway's cats given to him by a ship's captain. He purchased a fishing boat, the *Pilar,* and sailed with friends across the Caribbean. On the turquoise waters, Hemingway found inspiration for a new novel, *To Have and Have Not.* Set during the Great Depression, it describes the life of a Caribbean outlaw, lower-class violence, and upper-class corruption in Key West.

Hemingway named his cats after famous people, a tradition followed to this day.

In 1933, Hemingway and Pauline traveled to Africa on safari, visiting Kenya and the Serengeti. He wrote *Green Hill of Africa,* an account of big-game hunting, and *The Snows of Kilimanjaro,* where the main character, on safari, suffers an accident and must confront his own death. That same year his books, which in Germany were considered a tribute to modern decadence, were burned in Berlin.

In Nazi Germany, the German Student Union regularly burned books that were considered subversive or expressing views opposed to the regime.

On July 17, 1936, the Spanish Civil War began. Republicans fought and lost against fascist General Francisco Franco's nationalist group. This victory gave Franco control of Spain for the next thirty-six years. In early 1937, the North American Newspaper Alliance asked Hemingway to travel to Spain to report on the events. This was not his first encounter with fascism; in the 1920s he had interviewed the leader of the Italian National Fascist Party, Benito Mussolini, recognizing the ferocious dictator he was to become. Hemingway was deeply attached to Spain, its culture, customs, and people. He wrote articles and gave speeches to raise money to help the Republican cause. While in Spain, he worked with renowned Hungarian war photographer and photojournalist Robert Capa. *Life* magazine featured their collaboration. Hemingway wrote *The Fifth Column,* his only full-length play, set in besieged Madrid. His most impressive work, *For Whom the Bell Tolls,* was also inspired by his experience as a reporter during the Spanish Civil War. It was nominated for a Pulitzer Prize. Hemingway was joined in Spain by American journalist and war correspondent Martha Gellhorn, with whom he had been conducting a secret affair for several years.

Upon his return to America in 1939, Hemingway moved to Cuba. His house, a large farm named Finca Vigía, was located ten miles from Havana in the village of San Francisco de Paula. Hemingway decorated his home with African hunting trophies and other objects gathered during his safari, along with a small collection of paintings by renowned artists Joan Miró, Juan Gris, and Paul Klee. The library contained floor-to-ceiling shelves filled with hundreds of books. At that time, Hemingway distanced himself from Pauline, starting an agonizing and lengthy separation. Martha Gellhorn joined him in Cuba, and Hemingway and Pauline were divorced soon after. Pauline lived in Key West the rest of her life. She died in 1951, shortly after troubles with her son, Gregory, a substance abuser, and a heated

Finca Vigía translates to "Lookout Land" in English.

dispute over the phone with Hemingway.

Martha Gellhorn was born in 1908. Her father was a gynecologist with liberal views. Her mother, with whom she shared a close and loving relationship, was a suffragist and social activist. Like Hadley, Hemingway's first wife, Martha was a St. Louis native also educated at Bryn Mawr. She became a journalist and an accomplished fiction writer. Martha worked in France for a few years as one of the first female war correspondents before returning to America. She was a self-assured, nonconformist chain-smoker who enjoyed drinking and eating well. She traveled throughout the United States writing about the Depression for the Federal Emergency Relief Administration. Martha became Hemingway's third wife on December 20, 1940. They spent their summers in Ketchum, Idaho, and winters in Cuba on the property Hemingway loved to share with many cats.

War correspondents are required to report from war-torn areas of the world, which makes theirs the most dangerous type of journalism.

When World War II started, Hemingway took it upon himself to record in the *Pilar*'s day log his sightings of German U-boats cruising the Caribbean Sea. His second son, Patrick, often helped on improvised missions. Hemingway reported his findings to American intelligence officers. Now forty-four, Hemingway served as a correspondent during World War II. He flew several missions with the Royal Air Force and accompanied American troops as they landed on Omaha Beach on D-day. He later wrote: "I could see the first, second, third, fourth and fifth waves of landing troops lay where they had fallen, looking like so many heavily laden bundles on the flat pebbly stretch between the sea and first cover." Hemingway joined the Twenty-second Regiment and witnessed the liberation of Paris.

It took six days for the French forces, assisted by the U.S. Army, to liberate Paris from the German occupation.

Martha decided to join Hemingway in London, where he was now stationed. After a dangerous ocean crossing, she was reunited in the war-torn British capital with a husband who no longer loved her. Hemingway had met and fallen in love with American journalist and author Mary

Welsh, who was also working in London as a war correspondent. After four argumentative years of marriage, Martha and Hemingway divorced in 1945. She outlived him by almost forty years. Suffering from cancer, she committed suicide in 1998 in London.

Mary Welsh was born in 1908 in the lumbering, trading, and sawmill city of Walker, Minnesota, where her father was a lumberman. She had blue eyes, brown hair, and strong features and displayed a commanding confidence. Mary attended Chicago's Northwestern University, where she studied journalism. Twice married, she worked as a journalist at the *Chicago Daily News* and later moved to Paris as a correspondent for *Time* and *Life* magazines. After the German invasion of Paris, she relocated to London, where she worked for the *London Daily Express.* Hemingway married Mary, his fourth wife, in March 1946 in Cuba, where they lived until 1959.

In the early 1900s, most women journalists covered "society columns," where fashion, cooking, gardening, or parenting issues were addressed. Few women journalists reported on politics or war-related matters.

At a ceremony in 1947 at the U.S.

embassy in Cuba, Hemingway was awarded a Bronze Star for his service as a war correspondent. Following the war, a succession of accidents and health issues plagued the Hemingway family: He damaged his knee in a road accident; Mary suffered several broken bones while skiing; Patrick was injured in a traffic collision; depression fell upon Hemingway as many of his close friends began to die; years of heavy drinking resulted in acute headaches, weight issues, and high blood pressure. These unfortunate episodes, however, did not stop him from completing *The Garden of Eden* in five months.

Hemingway believed his eyelids were particularly thin, causing him to always wake at daybreak.

In 1948, while traveling in Italy with Mary, Hemingway, almost fifty, became infatuated with a beautiful eighteen-year-old Italian aristocrat, Adriana Ivancich. The platonic relationship lasted several years, with Adriana and Hemingway traveling together to Paris and Venice, exchanging letters when he returned to America, and Adriana staying with the Hemingway family while visiting Finca Vigía in Cuba.

Several of their letters are displayed at the JFK Presidential Library.

Clearly inspired by his relationship with his young muse, Hemingway composed a new novel, *Across the River and into the Trees.* Set in Venice at the end of the war, it reveals the bittersweet love story between an older American colonel and a young Italian countess. The book received terrible reviews. By 1955, the liaison with Adriana had concluded. In 1983, suffering from severe depression, Adriana hanged herself from a tree in her garden.

Hemingway decided to work on a new story following this literary fiasco. *The Old Man and the Sea,* a perfect depiction of courage in the face of defeat, was published originally in *Life* magazine and brought out subsequently in book form by Charles Scribner's Sons. The book was critically and commercially praised, selling more than 50,000 copies in a short period of time, assuring Hemingway financial stability. In 1953 Hemingway was awarded the Pulitzer Prize. President John F. Kennedy published his Pulitzer Prize–winning memoir, *Profiles in*

Courage, in 1955. JFK often expressed his admiration for Hemingway and in the opening sentence cited his description of courage: "This is a book about the most admirable of human virtues—courage. 'Grace under pressure,' Ernest Hemingway defined it."

Two years later and flush with money, Hemingway and Mary returned to Africa. Misfortune struck again. While flying over the Belgian Congo, the plane crash-landed and Hemingway suffered a head wound. The following day he boarded a plane to Uganda that exploded at takeoff, inflicting serious injuries: a severe concussion, cracked ribs, a liver tear, a ruptured kidney and spleen, and a disjointed arm and shoulder. After recovering, he sustained second-degree burns when a bushfire occurred while he was on a fishing trip with his family. To reduce the pain inflicted by these numerous injuries, Hemingway drank more heavily, aggravating his physical and mental condition.

Hollywood's Golden Age American actor Spencer Tracy received an Oscar nomination and a Golden Globe nomination for the adaptation of *The Old Man and the Sea.*

In October 1954, Hemingway was awarded the Nobel Prize in Literature. He gratefully accepted the award but, still in great pain from his recent injuries, decided not to travel to Sweden.

Two years later, he was reunited with trunks he had put in safekeeping at the Ritz Hotel in Paris in 1928. To his astonishment, Hemingway found journals he had written when he lived in Paris. Upon returning to Cuba, he organized his findings and proceeded to write his memoir, *A Moveable Feast*. The book included several personal accounts and never-before-published events of Hemingway's Parisian life, along with stories with his son Jack and first wife, Hadley. Also included were mocking observations of literary celebrities, such as F. Scott Fitzgerald, and interesting notes of Hemingway's own early trials with his art. What followed was an extremely busy period. Hemingway revised some of his previous writings, adding chapters to *The Garden of Eden*,

The memoir was published post-humously in 1964, three years after Hemingway's death.

lengthening *True at First Light,* and writing *Islands in the Stream.*

Hemingway agreed with Castro's overthrow of the Batista government, believing that the Cuban revolution was necessary. He and Mary decided to leave Finca Vigía in July 1960, however, after learning that Castro was going to nationalize property owned by foreign nationals. After the invasion of the Bay of Pigs in 1961, the property was confiscated by the Cuban government, along with Hemingway's extensive book collection. Hemingway and Mary moved permanently to Ketchum, Idaho, where they bought a home overlooking Big Wood River. The area offered fishing, shooting, and walking, reminding Hemingway of his youth in Michigan. He and Mary never returned to Cuba.

Led by the CIA to overthrow Fidel Castro and his Communist government, the Bay of Pigs invasion was launched from Central America and was defeated in three days by the Cuban armed forces.

After a short stay in Spain, where he was photographed for the cover of *Life* magazine, Hemingway suffered from anxiety, depression, and delusions. His mental health rapidly deteriorated, and he decided to return home to Idaho. Hereditary predispositions, chronic alcoholism, liver failure, diabetes, and multiple traumatic head injuries throughout his life contributed to his decline. Hemingway had accumulated a considerable fortune, which he mistakenly believed was mismanaged by his financial advisers. Paranoia set in as he believed he was being monitored by the FBI for imaginary tax fraud. Hemingway was hospitalized at the Mayo Clinic in Rochester, Minnesota, where he was diagnosed with bipolar disorder and received electroconvulsive therapy. After an unsuccessful additional treatment in early 1961, Hemingway was released from the clinic in worse condition than when first admitted, now suffering from severe amnesia. Three months later, he was admitted again after Mary found him in their kitchen, holding a gun. He received more electroshock therapy and returned home in June 1961, where his physical condition quickly deteriorated.

Patients treated with electroshock therapy receive a controlled electric current, causing brief seizures in the brain.

Like his father, Hemingway was diagnosed with hemochromatosis, a hereditary disease causing the body to absorb too much iron, creating mental and physical ailments. Hemingway's lifelong battle with alcoholism aggravated his condition. Braving adversity, Mary cared for him and remained by his side.

On July 2, 1961, two days after returning home, Hemingway killed himself in the entranceway of his house with a twelve-gauge double-barreled shotgun. He was sixty-one. Mary initially said that his death was accidental, but in an interview in 1966 she acknowledged that he had been mentally ill and that he had committed suicide.

Hemingway is buried at Ketchum Cemetery. Believing that his death was accidental, the local Catholic priest performed the funeral. A memorial was placed above Trail Creek, in nearby Sun Valley. Hemingway had written the engraved tribute for a friend who had died decades earlier:

Five Hemingway family members, over four generations, committed suicide: Hemingway, his father, his sister Ursula, his brother Leicester, and his granddaughter Margaux.

BEST OF ALL HE LOVED THE FALL
THE LEAVES YELLOW ON COTTONWOODS
LEAVES FLOATING ON TROUT STREAMS
AND ABOVE THE HILLS
THE HIGH BLUE WINDLESS SKIES
...NOW HE WILL BE A PART OF THEM
FOREVER

Upon Hemingway's death, President Kennedy noted: "Few Americans have had a greater impact on the emotions and attitudes of the American people than Ernest Hemingway.... He almost single-handedly transformed the literature and the ways of thought of men and women in every country in the world." After the death of JFK, letters between Mary Hemingway and Jacqueline Kennedy trace the decision to archive Hemingway's materials at the new John F. Kennedy Presidential Library. Jacqueline Kennedy announced the gift, noting the collection would "help to fulfill our hope that the Library will become a center for the study of American civilization, in all its aspects, in these years."

The Hemingway Room at the JFK Presidential Library features a mounted antelope head from a safari in 1933 and a lion-skin rug.

In 1965, Mary Hemingway created the Hemingway Foundation, whose mission is to advance the written word and promote emerging writers. The Hemingway Society was later established, supporting and developing Hemingway scholarship. Mary died in New York City in 1986. Her will requested that she be buried next to Hemingway in Ketchum.

The degree of Hemingway's impact is also clearly visible on popular culture. In 1978, Russian scientists discovered a small planet and named it 3656 Hemingway in his honor. *Wrestling Ernest Hemingway,* a 1993 movie about a friendship between two men, Irish and Cuban, starred Shirley MacLaine, Sandra Bullock, and Robert Duvall. The fine writing instruments company Montblanc created a Hemingway fountain pen. Multiple bars inspired by *Across the River and into the Trees* are called "Harry's" and many restaurants "Hemingway." Hemingway's first son, Jack, sponsored a line of furniture pieces including a “Kilimanjaro” table and a “Catherine” sofa.

Hemingway liked to depict strong, unsophisticated characters whose courage, trustworthiness, and decency are set against the ruthless system of modern society. He left behind a remarkable literary oeuvre that is still inspiring today’s writers. Ernest Hemingway is considered one of the greatest American novelists of the twentieth century.